The Microcosm
in the Macrocosm

The Word of the Stars to the Person, the Microcosm, and His Soul

Gabriele

A companion text for the book
"The Speaking All-Unity.
The Word of the Universal Creator-Spirit"

The WORD
The UNIVERSAL SPIRIT

First Edition July 2014
Published by:
© Universal Life - The Inner Religion
P.O. Box 3549, Woodbridge, CT 06525
U S A

Licensed edition
translated from the original German title:
"Der Mikrokosmos im Makrokosmos
Das Wort der Sterne an den Menschen, den
Mikrokosmos, und an seine Seele"
From the Universal Life Series
with the consent of
© Gabriele-Verlag Das Wort GmbH
Max-Braun-Str. 2, 97828 Marktheidenfeld
Germany

Order No. S175 en
The German edition is the work of reference for all
questions regarding the meaning of the content.

All rights reserved

ISBN 978-1-890841-12-6

Table of Contents

A walk on a starlit night 5

*All those who disdain God's
law of love and love for neighbor
are warriors against the law of God* 32

Help from the world of the stars! 35

A walk on a starlit night

When people look into the clear firmament of the evening, then every so often, one hears a joyous call like, for instance: "Oh, the stars – how unbelievably many stars and countless Milky Ways! Stars upon stars and suns upon suns, but the moon just can't go missing either."

Are we human beings aware that the material macrocosm provides the memory bank for every person, because his small world is stored there as a likeness? The material macrocosm and beyond that, the finer-material spheres, also called cosmoses, store all the important contents of our five components, feeling, sensing, thinking, speaking and acting. According to the movements and connections of certain planetary constellations, these send to the person only what he – the microcosm – entered into the macrocosm.

From a scientific point of view, no energy is lost. What each person sends out – positive or negative – comes back to him. Consequently, the echo in the person, that which befalls him, is the word of the stars, which, as already stated, store the inputs of each person and, according to the planetary or star constellation, send these back in segments to the person concerned.

Even though from time to time, we human beings hear or read that each of us is the microcosm in the macrocosm and a part of the material cosmos, many brush this aside, thinking: "Well, so what? And yet, the early Egyptians interpreted the signs of the stars as signs of the zodiac." – Seen as a whole, this makes sense, because the data in the stars leads to culmination points, which give our inputs back to each of us.

*

How can this be understood, that the word of the stars is reflected in each person, that is, that it radiates back and becomes apparent in or on the person, according to the planetary constellation in which some of our inputs are stored?

To understand these correlations, we have to assume that everything, absolutely everything, is based on energy, and that no energy is lost. Whether we think of the physical body, the human being, or of all that the Earth bears, such as animals, plants, trees, bushes, flowers, stones, mineral sources, and so on. – everything is based on energy and every consciousness aspect communicates with the same and similar aspects, because like always attracts like.

Animals, plants, trees, bushes, flowers and minerals are and remain unburdened. Their consciousness, which is also the life, is in communication with their Creator, the All-One, the Eternal One.

Nevertheless, all external material forms of the nature kingdoms are recorded in the material world of the stars, the macrocosm.

The soul in the person, however, is in communication, on the one hand, with the unburdened Being, the Kingdom of God, and, on the other, with its burdens in the finer-material spheres and in the material macrocosm, and this, according to the severity of the burden.

Man as such is the only living being on the planet Earth that can burden himself day after day, and that, as stated, with the negative content of his feeling, sensing, thinking, speaking and acting.

The energy a person emits first goes into the memory of his human brain, into his conscious mind and subconscious, as well as into the memory bank of the material cosmos and into the finer-material spheres. According to these inputs, the corresponding body cells are shaped via the brain.

From this, the person develops, the microcosm in the macrocosm. Consequently, every person is registered many times from the top of his head to the soles of his feet, as is his soul.

It is written: *Are not two sparrows sold for a penny? And not one of them will fall to the ground without your Father's will. But even the hairs on your head are numbered.*

From this, we can recognize that man is the microcosm in the macrocosm and in addition, his soul's aura finds its echo in the All-cosmos and in the finer-material spheres.

No mote of energy is lost. Day after day, each person prepares his own way himself, and is the architect of his fate. And so, what goes out from him also goes back into him and into his soul. When the person passes away, then the soul leaves its house, the microcosm. The finer-material body, the astral body, the soul, remains what the person was, for, as stated, no sowing is lost.

And so, what the person sows he also transmits to his soul.

When we consider that the smallest component in infinity is based on energy, then everything is also oriented to "sending and receiving," because energy – be it only a speck of dust – bears the germ of life. Life gives and receives. Consequently, in the All, the cosmos, even the smallest energetic volume has its corresponding receiver.

And so, in all of infinity, there is nothing static; everything, absolutely everything, is in movement; everything sends and has its specific receiver.

The bookkeeping of infinity is limitless. The "debit" or "credit" of every single one of us – whether human being or his soul – is meticulously recorded.

Everything negative that the person has not rectified, including what concerns his past, is in communication with the material cosmos, with the energetically like-vibrating planetary constellations. Beyond this, as stated, his soul is also registered in finer-material spheres.

Many, very many, people hardly think about the fact that what they radiate is energy and that at some point it will go back into them, because no energy is lost, and energy – whether positive or negative – emits. Whoever emits it receives. So it can be said that whatever comes to the person each day is his inputs in the stars. And so, the stars store the content of our behavior patterns and send these to us in the most varying situations and occurrences. As a result, each individual person receives what he has input into the stars and planets.

Therefore, at every instant, every second and every minute, each person is in communication with the material macrocosm, and his soul, with the finer-material spheres as well, which, among other things, point out to it the path to the next higher levels.

As frequently stated, the material universe's ocean of stars of formed via the Fall-thought of wanting to be greater than the All-One, who is called God in the western world. The Fall developed from the impure roots of the principle "divide, bind and rule," as opposed to the divine principle of unity "link and be."

And so, density, which we call matter, formed through the estrangement from the law of God, which is love, equality and unity. The macrocosm merged and merges into cascade-like structures, into light-poor energetic waves, a kind of surge that, over unimaginable cycles, piled and pile up, wave-like, into energetic quantities, that is, that merged and merge into similar masses, and at that, with differing light intensity.
According to human concepts, we call the energetically piled-up, light-poor masses the material cosmos.
The material cosmos is nothing more than the dross of the Fall-beings. All generations of human beings and their souls have their share in this. Looking deeper, we can deduce from this the reincarnation of many souls.
The low point of human ignorance is the ego of today's generations and it is the declaration of

war against God, for God, the Eternal, is the all-giving love and the love for neighbor, the law of unity and equality.

The mighty Kingdom of God is fine-material and everything that lives and is active in the Kingdom of God is fine-material, that is, primordial substance; it is the eternal law of love for God and neighbor. In the Kingdom of God, it is the divine beings; it is the All-creation-life of the spiritual minerals, plants, animals and nature beings. All in all, it is the power, the life, the love of the mighty All-Creator-Spirit.
The creating and drawing eternal law of the All-One, the infinite, eternal, inexhaustible fullness of the eternal Being, is effective in all of infinity. All cosmoses, also the material cosmos, are embedded in the inexhaustible law of infinity.

We read of the Fall of the rebellious beings, whose striving and aspiration was to dissolve all divine forms, including the Kingdom of God. In the process, their light intensity decreased more and more, with the result that their bodies became darker and coarser.

Instead of returning to the eternal divine kingdom, they used up – that is, abused – their light-potential more and more. Despite perceiving this, they continued to fight against the law of love for God and neighbor, against the law of All-Unity.

After each fight against the law of God, against the unity of the eternal Kingdom of God, they noticed that light-poor zones developed. It was energies and structures that were becoming ever coarser, and which corresponded to their energetically light-poor existence.

Gradually the rebellious beings realized that their volume of energy was diminishing, because their bodies became denser material.

In cycles, in which the Fall-thought proceeded, it became discernible that they needed a so-called base, to further act against the All-law, against the law of God. According to the Fall-volume that corresponded to them, they sought a point of sojourn in one of the already existing finer-material spheres, from which they could continue their fight against the All-Unity, against the Kingdom of God.

In countless thrusts of the Fall, the material cosmos emerged from this, a mass of light-poor heavenly bodies pushed together, of which the Earth is also one, which the rebellious beings had chosen as base, that is, a military base, which they structured accordingly.

In cycles of condensation from the former divine spiritual energy to the material cosmic dross of the Fall, the material cosmos, coarse-material forms developed in further thrusts of energy, which ultimately led to the development of human beings.

The Fall-thought is the reversed principle of equality, freedom, unity and brotherliness, that is, brotherli- sisterliness, and justice. From these five powers of unity, equality was turned into inequality; freedom into lack of freedom, which says: "I'll take the liberty to do that"; unity was turned into disunity, which says: "I'm my own best friend!"; brotherliness, that is, brotherli- sisterliness, was turned into the lack of brotherli- sisterliness, into egoism; and justice was turned into injustice, assertiveness.

These negative warfare agents contain all-too-human associations in an individual's feeling, sensing, thinking, speaking and acting, whereby thoughts are the most dangerous warfare agent. Thoughts that come from the customary feelings and sensations are the precursors of corresponding deeds.

The picture, which crystallizes from the content of feelings and sensations, emerges in thoughts. The picture – whether it has a positive or negative basis – will become effective at some point, because it goes into the stars and planets, and from there, it comes into effect according to cosmic courses of events.

And so, what a person sends is what he receives. Seed and harvest remain inseparable until they are rectified by the sender, the person. To be able to better understand the energetic correlations that are beyond the scope of the material cosmos, we should realize that the person is nothing more than the shell of a being that is called soul, in the very basis of which a fine-material being that belongs to the Kingdom of God acts and reacts. A person can burden his soul up to the essential light-force that is in the very basis of the soul of each person, also called the core of being; the core of being itself, however, is incorruptible.

When the shell, the person, passes on, the soul disincarnates. The soul's place of residence can then be the material cosmos or finer-material spheres. This depends solely on the extent to which the soul is shadowed, on the corresponding light intensity of the former human being. The soul's shell, the person, is thus the decisive factor in terms of what he encumbers himself and his soul with.

The cosmic bookkeeping is precise. The "debit" and "credit" of the person and his soul are in constant communication with the All and are recorded in the All.

The material macrocosm moves according to the sending and receiving volume of all human beings. This results in the consolidation of planets that have stored the same and similar inputs. They are culmination points of sending volumes, which, among other things, affect people who have something to clear up with each other, and to whom a message is sent on ahead. The sending and receiving volume from the corresponding cosmic culmination points of energy always correspond to the "debit" and "credit" of the person and his soul.

At every moment, the "debit" and "credit" is decisive; it weighs and measures. The person's past that he has not worked off is the future of his soul.

Every person is the architect of his fate. No person can force his energy onto another. What each individual emits he will also rightfully receive, himself.

It is written that man should not deceive himself, for he will reap what he sows. The material macrocosm and the finer-material spheres are storage cosmoses. According to iron laws, every seed that has not been dealt with will sprout at some point.

A person should think much more often about God's just bookkeeping, and that each person receives only what he has sown – and not what another sows in regard to him. This means that what others negatively think, speak or even do regarding us is their seed and also their harvest, unless we have a share in it. Through this, we create our causes, which at some point become effective in us. If we are linked with the other person through mutually created causes, then each one is hit by what he sowed or thought, spoke or even did toward the other.

And so, the effects in the person, the harvest, can vary. They always correspond to the person's inputs. A culmination point radiates out and hits people who form a root in the causal network; they will receive only their share of this.

Each day, we should realize more often that it doesn't depend on whether what we feel, sense, think and say is correct. It depends solely on the content of what is contained in these five components, that is, what we put into them.

What comes to every one of us human beings is not a coincidence. Only that comes to us which we ourselves have entered into the world of the stars, into the macrocosm.

As stated, the countless material stars and planets, whether we see them or not, are memory banks as are the finer-material spheres, also called cosmoses. In every memory bank is the Eternal, God, the All-love, the kindness and mercy.

God, the love, is not a punishing God, who radiates His inputs via the ocean of stars to the person without advance warnings and hints. God is the admonition and the help in our conscience, insofar as this is intact, which means, it is not occupied by Earth-bound forces.

An example: A developing culmination point first begins to admonish and warn all those people who are under the radiation intensity of a developing culmination point. Admonitions and warnings frequently announce themselves via the events of the day.

Depending on the inputs, the eternal power, God's love, admonishes and gives warnings via the world of stars, and points out many a thing in an intact conscience, for example, certain indispositions, small or even larger personal unpleasantness at work, on the street, during a drive, while shopping or in the family between wife and husband, with the children, with relatives, and so on. These are always hints, admonitions and warnings, which the love, kindness and mercy, the omnipresence of God has come to us.

God admonishes; God warns; God helps.
Unfortunately, most admonitions and hints are viewed as "coincidence" or shrugged off with the words "The other is to blame!" or "I was

lucky today!" or "The doctor's diagnosis is not serious."

A higher dose of radiation from the world of stars, from the culmination point that is coalescing, can trigger a blow of fate or even an illness and much more. But the love for God and neighbor is always the timely admonishing and helping force.

Among other things, the material stars are also guides, if our sending volume is largely positive and corresponds to the Ten Commandments of God through Moses, as well as to the teachings of the Sermon on the Mount of Jesus. From this, the positive powers in us unfold. Then we can receive help from God's omnipresent law of love, kindness and mercy.

An alert wayfarer on the path over this Earth is aware that nothing happens by chance and that everything has something to say to us. But he also knows that a higher power supports and helps him, so that with the power of Christ, he can repent of and clear up in time what is threatening to break out in the way of negative aspects. And if he no longer strives for this and similar things, it is nullified and transformed into the positive.

In the past of each person there are many fingers that point out what can be rectified in time, for example, envy, quarrel, jealousy, hatred, denigration of others, family strife, but also mobbing at work and much more.

*

In each of us is the strength to recognize what is not good, what is against the law of God, so as to rectify it before some of it becomes effective – provided we are willing to question ourselves, to see ourselves, warts and all, in terms of what might be going on with us.

If we have found the starting point of our dangerous seed, then it is much easier for us to change our way of thinking and create a positive image of humanity.

In the process, the words of Jesus could help us: *Come to terms quickly with your accuser while you are going with him to court, lest your accuser hand you over to the judge, and the judge to the guard, and you be put in prison. Truly, I say to you, you will never get out until you have paid the last penny.*
Many a one asks: "Why clear things up with my opponent as long as I am on the way with him, that is, in the temporal?"

Let us think about the following: Feelings, sensations, thoughts, words and deeds can be compared to bowls or shells. Each person places in the bowl, or shell, different concepts of a personal kind, which he is not always able to grasp and see through in the rapidity of the events of the day. And yet, they are energies produced by the person, which he stores in himself, in his soul and in the world of stars.
And so, the five components have contents that are decisive without exception, because, on the one hand, they shape our body, the cells and

organs, and, on the other, they are absorbed, that is, stored, by the material cosmos, and beyond that, by finer spheres of extraterrestrial cosmoses.

As stated, when the physical body, the person, passes on, then the soul leaves its house, that is, its body, and takes the path in the world of stars that the person has transmitted to it.

And so, the person is the seismograph of his soul. A more light-filled soul takes the path of forgetting into higher, finer-material spheres. A shadowed, that is, light-poor, soul that is close to the Earth may remain bound to the material cosmos, because it is still Earth-bound.
The person's world of programs, the content of which is the five components, is decisive.
Particularly in today's materialistic times, man exposes himself without thought to many world-oriented offers.
With this, he burdens himself and his soul, which can be Earth-bound after the demise of his physical body, because the materialistic

dream world is an imprint in the person and in the soul, which, after leaving its body, strives again and again to incarnate, that is, to embody itself, in order to live out its desires and addictions as a human being.
We human beings should realize more often that like always attracts like and like draws to like.

Another variation presents itself to an Earth-bound soul when no incarnation is possible:
In this case, it looks for people with the same unfulfilled desires and abnormal addictions. It sneaks into the auras of those people who live in the same condition as the Earth-bound soul, in order to get and fulfill for itself through the person what the latter is lusting for.

Despite all these dangers, the Earth is a place of grace, for every person is warned in time by the Eternal, by God, via the stars and planets, so that he may repent of, clear up and no longer do the un-good. In this way, the person and his soul can free themselves from their burdens and from being spiritually bound to the Earth. Thus, every individual can achieve unimaginably much that is positive for himself and for his soul.

If the person did not make use of his time on Earth, then it's possible that after its disembodiment the soul remains close to the Earth, for the negative aspects that have not yet been worked off are the future of the person and his soul. In places of expiation, in culmination points of stars and planets, the soul then often has to most painfully expiate what the person inflicted on it and is active in it.

A request to clear things up is not readily possible like it is on matter among people. The paths in the cosmoses are totally different for each soul. For this reason, it's not always so easily possible to reach a soul in another soul region or even the human being concerned, to rectify the current negative aspect that is active in the soul.

How often, after a dangerous incident or an illness we have recovered from, do we hastily and casually think or say: "I just squeaked by that fairly well!" Mostly it remains with this statement. One continues to act as before.

Unfortunately, few people ask themselves: "What does that want to tell me?" For what has not been rectified remains in the repository stars.

It's possible that the material cosmos has stored even more things, but only the very fewest think about this. The undemanding person is satisfied that he just "squeaked by," as he says. The warnings from the culmination point were, however, not heeded and the causes were not rectified. Quite the contrary: The person continues to think, speak and act as before. This means that he continues to enter his negative seeds into the repository stars.

At the given time, the stated culmination point will again radiate to the person what is stored in the culmination point, and it will be only that which the person has inflicted on himself, because postponed is not cancelled.

What the individual person has entered into the world of the stars as negative aspects can be cancelled only by himself, because no other person has access to the contents of the feelings, sensations, thoughts, words and actions of another.

*

The earthly existence is a chance for every person and his soul.
In the temporal, a person can go to a physician to have his indisposition or illness treated. In addition, he can go to court to demand, even to dispute, his rights.
All this is not possible in the beyond. After the disembodiment of the soul, clearing things up happens primarily through expiation. In the beyond, there is no physician who prescribes medications for the soul. In the beyond, there is no earthly court or administration of justice. The repository stars are the court of justice; they weigh and measure and allocate to each person his portion of the wrong. And so, in all

the infinity of existence in the beyond, there is no law and no administration of justice, no one-sided condemnation. The bookkeeping of God, the cosmoses, forms the scales that very precisely plumbs everything and justly allocates accordingly to the soul its part.

Thus, the burdened soul in the beyond has it much harder than the human being does on this side of life.

If we are prudent, then we realize that many people have a good life at the expense of others. They don't think about what they inflict on their fellowman. After leaving its body, such a soul is upset, disappointed and aggressive, because it can't achieve what it could as a human being. World-bound egomaniac souls stay in the material cosmos for a long time, because they lack the desire for spiritual maturity. Many of these souls stay close to the Earth and press to become human beings again, that is, to incarnate anew.

As already stated: Whatever the person has inflicted on his soul is stored in the material cosmos and in the finer-material stars and planets. Because it is as it is, the possibility can be radiated to each soul either to continue the path to the finer-material stars or to consider another incarnation, provided that this possibility is given.

To repeat: We frequently read and hear about Fall-beings that turned away from the divine All-law, in order to conquer the Kingdom of God, to bring about its Fall and to found their own realm that corresponds to their concepts. Through their measures, these divine beings shadowed themselves more and more and in myriad windows of time fell ever deeper, through which they enveloped themselves with their negative energies. In passages of time that we human beings cannot measure, the human body developed. Embodiment and thus, incarnation resulted from the principle of shadowing and condensation. In myriad windows of time, the re-embodiment of the soul developed, the repeated incarnation.

*All those who disdain God's
law of love and love for neighbor
are warriors against the law of God*

When we compare mankind of today with earlier generations, then the belligerent behavior against man and nature is consistently visible. Crimes, wars, famines, including pestilences, pass from generation to generation. Today's mankind thinks it is more enlightened than past generations.

Formerly, much was done in secret; people covered things up and kept quiet. Today things are much more open; things are done without thinking about the fact that ultimately, one is a warrior against God's All-love.

What frequently took place long ago in secret were similar methods as today. For example, to many, the Middle Ages are long past. Let us ask ourselves whether today's methods aren't similar, except that they are openly covered up, by being clothed in the cloak of the "defense" of a country and the starving people are equipped with a begging system, whereby the folk is called on to donate. What do the governments of the so-called prosperous countries do? They ask the folk to pay up. In the face of this begging, the state pays billions every year to the surfeited rich churches in Germany.

These correlations make it clear that in a "humane" way, the hungry are kept at arms length and made to starve. Today more or less sugarcoated methods are used. In former generations, it was, as stated, dungeons, prisons, burning at the stake and not lastly, wars – often at command of the church with its Crusades and crusaders, which massacred the people, yes, whole nations, and that, in the name of Jesus, the Christ. Today, everything is sugarcoated and prudently weighed, in order to present the folk with the side that says: "Donate, donate, pay taxes and pay again."

At all times the churches have required their faithful to "eat humble pie" and become members, in order to make their small donation to the "cross" – in reality, the "cross" that is the problem with the church.

If we consider that everything is energy – whether positive, that is, God-conscious, or "sanctimoniously positive," that is, "sugarcoated with God" – then we should be aware that not one iota of energy is lost. All energy that goes out from us comes back into us. At some point, the culmination point is reached in the world of the stars. Then the aspects that we, the person, have entered hit us.

Once more in summary, this means that in light of the memory banks in the material cosmos, all non-expiated, negative energies have to be transformed, at that, either by the person or after his demise, by the discarnate soul.
The cosmoses are not bound to time. The cosmic irradiation corresponds to the individual's inputs. When and how these become effective in the person's life is decided by each one himself.

Help from the world of the stars!

When, for instance, a person is addressed by second or third parties about his negative behavior patterns, he is usually outraged. The outrage brings his nervous system into turmoil, which is noticeable in his central nervous system.

The outrage contains a message. It wants to communicate with us. If we question ourselves on this, we learn what is in the depths of our five components.
Who are we? And where will we be when our soul leaves its house, the body, which was its vehicle for this side of life?

Everything, absolutely everything, wants to tell us something.
Our nervous system can be compared to a seismograph. When we get upset about others and perhaps pay them back in kind, then the seismograph, our tense nervous system, signals

somewhat more strongly. It is upset, because we do not grasp that it wants to convey a message to us from the world of the stars.

There are so many people on Earth, because the apathy of many people has surrendered the measure of all things and situations to the secular and ecclesiastical authorities. When we watch ourselves and our fellow humans, we recognize that a large number of people are occupied with trifles and that a group of people has turned away from God, the Eternal, surrounding people with sugarcoated and spiritually underhanded methods and a belligerent personal network of machinations.

Another lasso on the part of the churches is a belief system that essentially says that belief without divine works is enough. – However, divine works can be done only when the content of our feeling, sensing, thinking and speaking is largely in agreement with the All-law of love for God and neighbor. Everything else that is made of the word "belief" is part of church doctrine.

The following statement draws through mankind like a Fata Morgana: "I believe in God, our heavenly Father, and in Christ, our Redeemer." If belief as such were enough, without works of selfless love for God and neighbor, then in our world, there would be no wars, fewer blows of fate, no famines, and our Mother Earth with its animals and nature would breathe a sigh of relief. A belief without the step-by-step fulfillment of the Ten Commandments of God and of the teachings of Jesus of Nazareth and His Sermon on the Mount is a Fata Morgana, a dead faith.

It is convenient to follow the doctrines of church leaders, because you don't have to think about it when it's said that belief alone is enough.

Let's look the facts in the eye: No person, not church leaders either, can rectify our negative energies – not even if we believe in church doctrinal statements and close our eyes when it's said to look at ourselves, or before the hunger in this world or before the animal torture and the murder of animals or when nature suffers under the urge-driven excesses of tearing down everything for the sake of egoism, because faith alone is enough and one affected to be "more intelligent" than God.

A question to the reader: Where does the dependency of many people come from, when God, the Eternal, gave to every person the free will of self-decision and the responsibility for what he does or does not do?
Free will is in God and in the very basis of our soul, because we are sons and daughters of God in the very basis of our soul.
Because according to His law, that is, His Order, God, the Eternal, conveyed to each person free will, which is inherent in the very basis of each soul, every single one of us is also himself responsible for what he does or does not do, himself.
In order to get out of the dilemma of dependencies, God gave the people the Ten Com-

mandments through Moses, excerpts from the law of the Kingdom of God, and Jesus gave us the teaching of the heavens, the Sermon on the Mount. That is the way to a higher life – and there is no other way.

The church institutions have their dogmas, rituals, traditions and ecclesiastical laws, which apply to those people who believe in the church and worship a God of the church.
God, the Eternal, is freedom, the all-encompassing eternal love and love of neighbor. His Spirit is not active in any tradition, in any ritual, any church law or dogma. God is freedom and the free Spirit is active in all of infinity and in the very basis of the soul of every person.
Each day, the person himself decides about his life on Earth and the development of his soul.
Read and check it out! You are free in your belief.

*

Dear fellow people, belief here, belief there, every external religion has its beliefs, but there is only one God, exclusively. No matter what religion wants to bring a belief home to you, it is and remains a Fata Morgana if one should merely believe without deeds.

No human being, not I, Gabriele, either, can prove to you that God, the almighty Spirit, dwells in you, and that you can experience God in the very basis of your soul, that is, in yourself.

A person in the Spirit of truth should activate his faith, by doing, step by step, what God, the Eternal, taught him through Moses, and Jesus, the Christ, in His Sermon on the Mount.

If in time we experience that God dwells in us, in every person, then for one thing, we have a prospect for our life, and for another, a goal that is called active faith.

Each one of us is asked whether he is striving to experience God in himself, or whether he wants to leave it to others, for example, to the churchmen who preach the passive faith. A simple example, taken from our daily life: A package arrives at your house. You say to yourself: "Oh yes, I believe that it contains what I ordered."

If you don't open the package, then it remains with the belief that it contains what you ordered.

Will you open the package when you assume that what you ordered is precious, or do you let the package with its valuable content be opened by someone else, who doesn't know the content that you value?

Dear fellow people, it's similar when we merely believe that God dwells in us and are not willing to open ourselves for Him, for God, for the precious in us.

We could compare ourselves to the wrapped package. We people need to open ourselves, by doing, step by step, what God taught us through Moses, in the Ten Commandments, and Jesus, in His Sermon on the Mount.

We, every single one of us, at some point have to find the valuable content, which is alive in us, which is the life in us. It is God, the light of the heavenly Father. None other can uncover for us the precious treasure in us. We alone have to do it.

Each of us knows that time rushes by ever faster and the hours fly. We could begin today and now to open the "package," ourselves, in order to draw closer to the precious content, God in us.

May I, Gabriele, encourage you to use your valuable days in the awareness: God in you, God in us?

Whoever makes an effort day after day to draw closer to the precious treasure in himself will experience on himself that he is changing more and more toward the positive. In time, he feels happier, freer and senses a certain kind of secureness that comes from within.

That could be a certain answer from God, our heavenly Father.

You yourself are called upon to activate your inactive faith, by letting it become a certainty

– God in you, God in every person, in nature, in the animal, in all of infinity. In time, you will change toward the positive; your feelings will become finer, your thoughts more light-filled and you will realize that God is love.

With cordial and heartfelt greetings,
Gabriele

The Speaking All-Unity

The Word of the Universal Creator Spirit

A Cosmic Work of Teaching and Learning from the School of Divine Wisdom

This work of cosmic teaching and learning ingeniously and outstandingly explains what religion, philosophy and science since their inception cannot comprehensibly explain – the great spiritual correlations of life.

Have you ever wondered, for example, that wild geese can fly in perfect formation? Doesn't this show that they must have a communication system that is far superior to us human beings? We have developed a technology that helps us to communicate over long distances, however, this technology is only a pale reflection of the All-communication.

"The Speaking All-Unity," a Cosmic Work of Teaching and Learning from the School of Divine Wisdom, leads us into the dimensions of the All-communication that connect all living beings and lifeforms. We learn, with the help of various exercises, for example, on a virtual walk, to refine our sensations towards the creation of God and to perceive more consciously the life in all Being.

384 pp., Hardbound, Includes an Audio-CD with 2 beautiful meditations from the divine consciousness:
"Everything Is in Bloom" and "Our True Being"
Order No. S173en, ISBN: 978-1-890841-33-1, $29.00 + S+H